French - Persian

LEARNING FLASHCARDS

FOR BABIES TODDLERS

alligator

تمساح

The alligator is having a party.

fourmi

مورچه

The ant is red.

ours

خرس

The bear loves you.

abeille

زنبور عسل

The bee is saying hello.

oiseau

پرنده

The bird is flying.

papillon

پروانه

The butterfly is pretty.

chameau

شتر

The camel has a hump.

chat

گربه

The cat is happy.

dinosaure

دایناسور

The dinosaur is laying eggs.

poulet

جوجه

The chicken is dancing.

vache

گاو

The cow has a bell.

cerf

گوزن

The reindeer has a toy.

chien

سگ

The dog has two floppy ears.

dauphin

دلفين

The dolphin is swimming.

canard

اردک

The duck has a bow.

aigle

عقاب

The eagle is looking for food.

l'éléphant

فيل

The elephant is sitting.

poisson

ماهى

The fish is a clownfish.

libellule

سنجاقک

The dragonfly is blue.

renard

روباه

The fox has a red nose.

grenouille

قورباغه

The frog is smiling.

girafe

زرافه

The giraffe has a long neck.

chèvre

بز

The goat has a beard

ver de terre

کرم

The worm is in the apple

poule

مرغ

The hen has chicks.

hippopotame

اسب ابی

The hippo is big.

cheval

اسب

The horse is fast.

kangourou

کانگورو

The kangaroo has a baby.

chaton

بچه گربه

The kitten is playing.

lion

شیر نر

The lion has a mane.

homard

خرچنگ

The lobster is red.

singe

میمون

The monkey has a tail.

poulpe

اختاپوس

The octopus has food.

hibou

جغد

The owls have big eyes.

panda

پاندا

The panda wears a diaper.

porc

خوک

The pig is fat and pink.

chiot

The dog is brown.

lapin

The rabbit has a carrot.

rat

The mouse is writing something.

crabe

The crab has two pinchers.

requin

The shark is scary.

mouton

The sheep are very fluffy.

escargot

حلزون

The snail is slow.

serpent

مار

The snake has poison.

araignée

عنكبوت

The spider is purple.

écureuil

سنجاب

The squirrel has a nut.

tigre

ببر

The tiger has a red bow.

tortue

لاک پشت

The turtle has a shell.

loup

گرگ

The wolf is smiling.

zèbre

گورخر

The zebra is black and white.

dinde

بوقلمون

The turkey has two legs.

coq

خروس

The rooster will crow.

perroquet

طوطی

The parrot is colorful.

hérisson

جوجه تیغی

The hedgehog has apples.

pomme

سیب

The apple has a leaf.

abricot

زردآلو

The apricot is yellow.

avocat

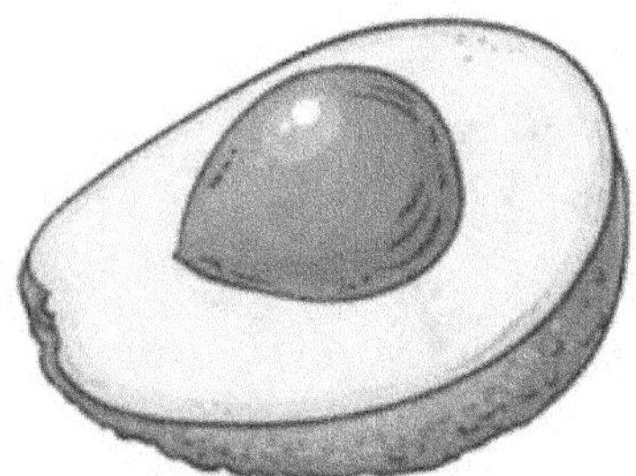

آووکادو

The avocado has a nut.

banane

موز

The banana is yellow.

la mûre

توت سیاه

There are a lot of blackberries.

cassis

سیاه دانه

The blackcurrants are yummy.

myrtille

زغال اخته

The blueberries are sweet.

cerise

گیلاس

The cherries have a stem.

noix de coco

نارگیل

The coconuts have juice.

figues

انجیر

The fig has seeds.

grain de raisin

انگور

The grapes are purple.

pamplemousse

گریپ فروت

The grapefruits are sour.

kiwi

کیوی

The kiwi is fresh.

citron

لیمو

The lemons are yellow.

citron vert

اهک

We have lots of lime.

litchi

لیچی

I like to eat lychee.

mandarine

پرتقال ماندارین

Oranges are refreshing.

mangue

انبه

Mango is my favorite fruit.

orange

نارنجی

Mandarins are like oranges.

papaye

پاپایا

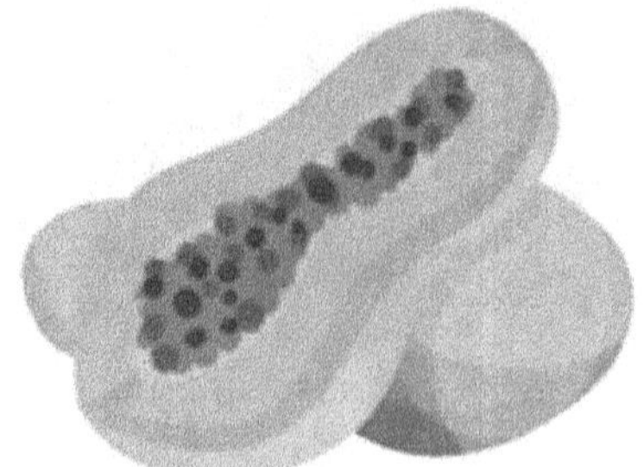

Papayas have lots of seeds.

pêche

هلو

Peaches are juicy.

poire

گلابی

Pears have a strange figure.

ananas

آناناس

The pineapple has a thumbs up.

prune

آلو

Plums are healthy for you.

grenade

انار

Pomegranates are all red.

framboise

تمشک

The raspberry is shiny.

fraise

توت فرنگی

The strawberry has leaves on top.

pastèque

هندوانه

The watermelon is big.

mandarine

نارنگی

The tangerine looks like an orange.

tarte

پای

I like to eat apple pie.

gâteau

کیک

That cake is huge.

bonbons

آب نبات

Candy is not good for your teeth.

biscuit

کوکی

Cookies are easy to make.

donut

دونات

I like strawberry donuts.

crème glacée

بستنی

The ice cream is melting.

muffin

کلوچه

The muffin has a cute wrapper.

pudding

پودینگ

We eat pudding on Christmas.

classeur

بند

I keep pictures in my binder.

livre

کتاب

I like to eat books.

sac à dos

کوله پشتی

The backpack has lots of stuff.

les ciseaux

قیچی

I have scissors in my bag.

épingles

پین

Pins can hold stuff up.

agrafe

کلیپ

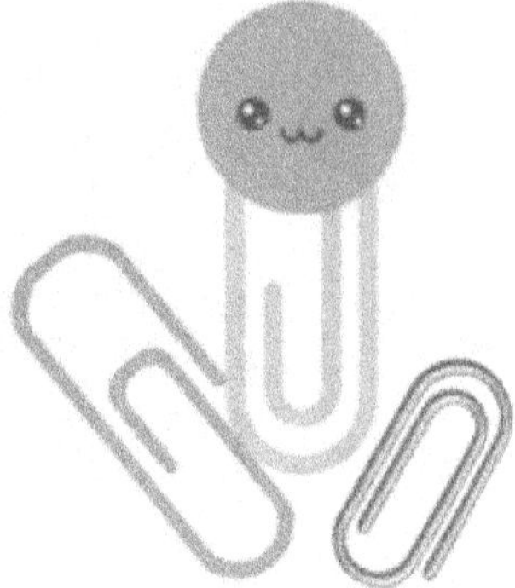

Clips can hold up paper.

papier

کاغذ

I have lots of paper.

agrafeuse

منگنه

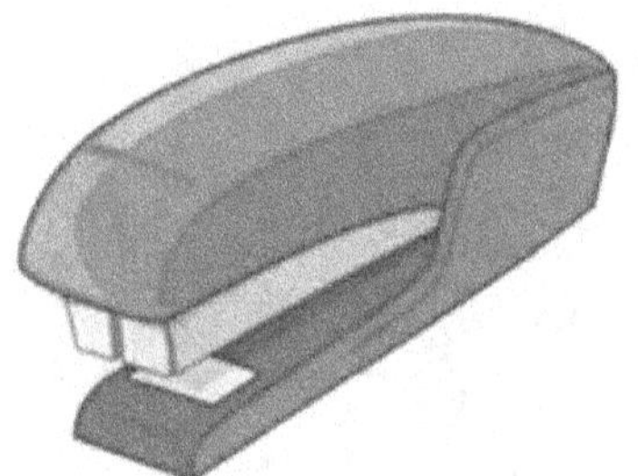

My stapler is shiny and red.

calculatrice

ماشین حساب

My calculator has buttons.

règle

خط کش

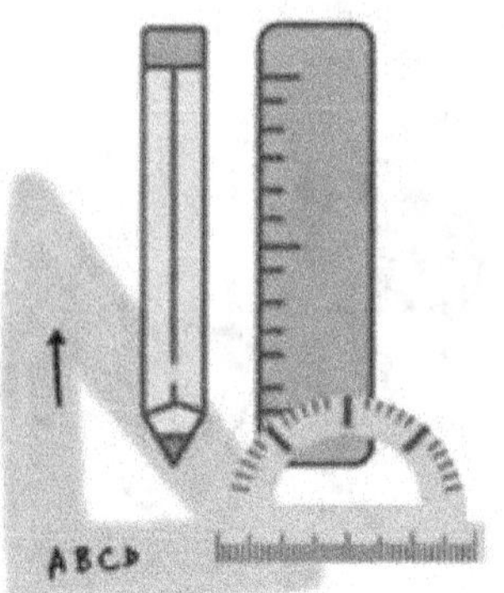

I have lots of rulers.

la colle

چسب

The glue is sticky.

bibliothèque

My bookcase has lots of things.

calendrier

I have a calendar on my table.

chaise

My chair is fancy.

l'horloge

The clock says that it's 3 o'clock.

ordinateur

I do things on my computer.

bureaux

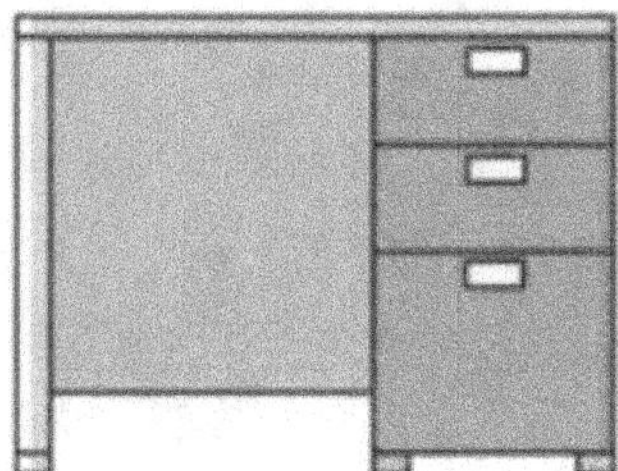

I put lots of things on my desk.

dictionnaire

فرهنگ لغت

The dictionary has lots of words.

la gomme

پاک کن

Erasers are used with pencils.

carte

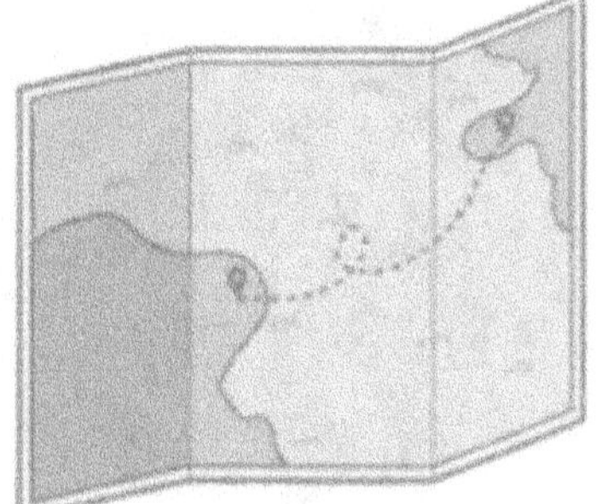

نقشه

The map shows you different places.

carnet

نوت بوک

I use notebooks at school.

stylo

خودکار

My pen is very pretty.

crayon

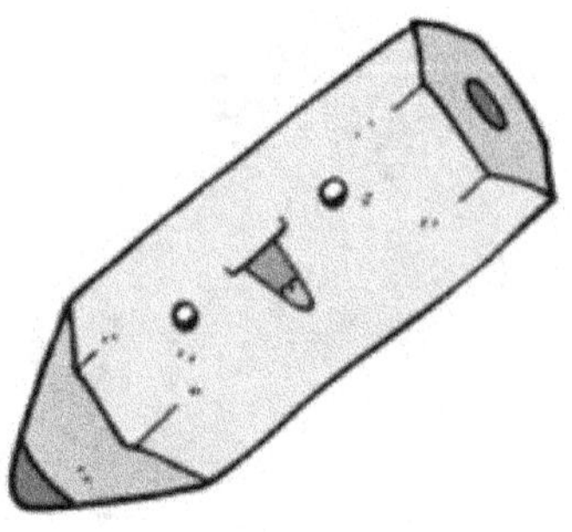

مداد

My friend gave me a pencil.

ceinture

کمربند

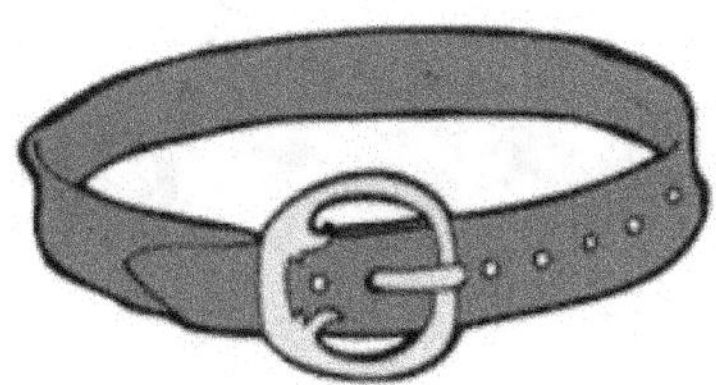

I have a belt on my pants.

bottes

چکمه

I have big brown boots.

chapeau

کلاه

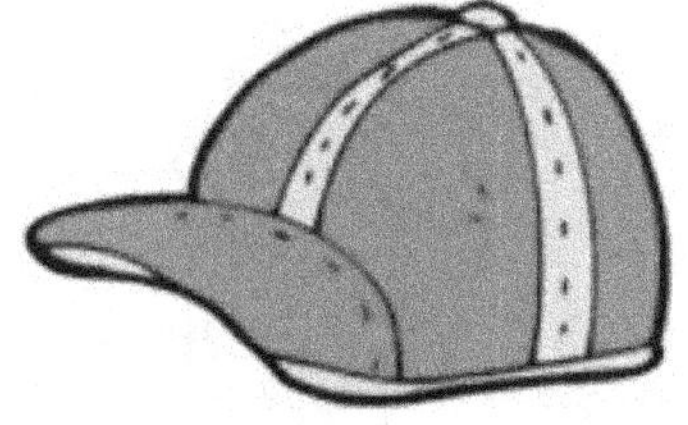

My mom bought me a new cap.

manteau

کت

She has a long yellow coat.

robes

لباس

My dress has a bow.

gants

دستکش

I got new gloves.

chapeau

كلاه

That hat is for a wicked witch.

veste

ژاکت

The jacket is cozy.

jeans

شلوار جین

My jeans are long.

pyjamas

لباس خواب

I sleep in my pajamas.

un pantalon

شلوار

The bear is wearing pants.

imperméable

لباس بارانی

We wear our raincoats when it is raining.

écharpe

روسری

The baby has a scarf around his neck.

chemise

پیراهن

I like this shirt the best.

des chaussures

کفش

I have red and blue shoes.

jupe

دامن

My skirt has lots of buttons.

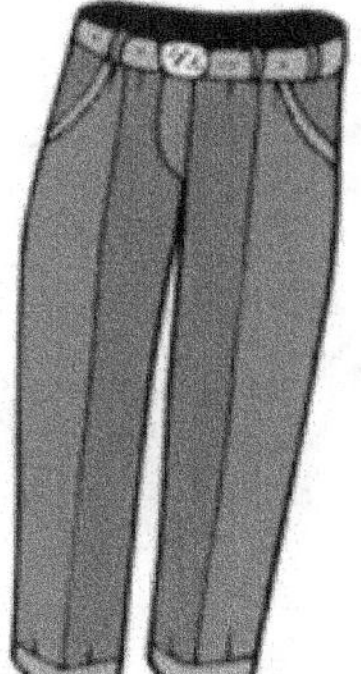

pantalon

برش

My dad wears slacks.

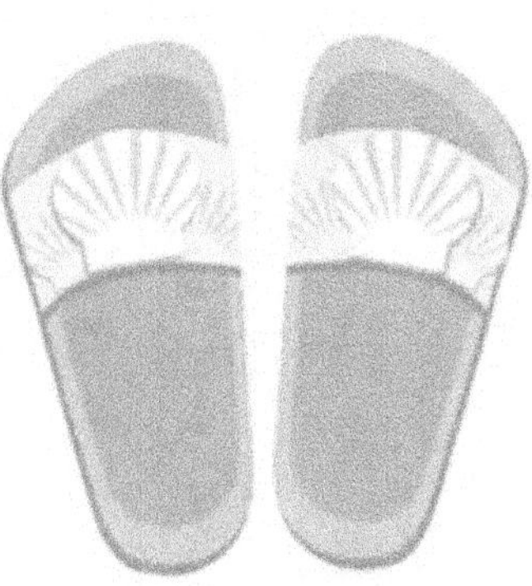

chaussons

دمپایی

I have seashells on my sandals.

chaussettes

جوراب

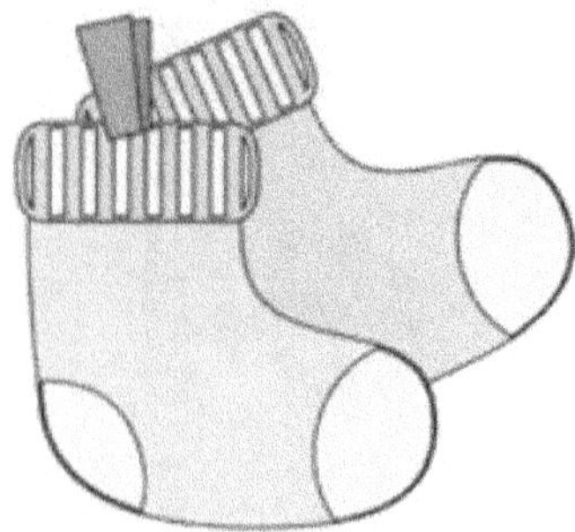

My baby sister wears socks.

costume

کت و شلوار

My brother is wearing a suit.

chandail

ژاکت

I am wearing a sweater for winter.

cravate

گردن

My dad wears a tie to meetings.

pantalon

شلوار

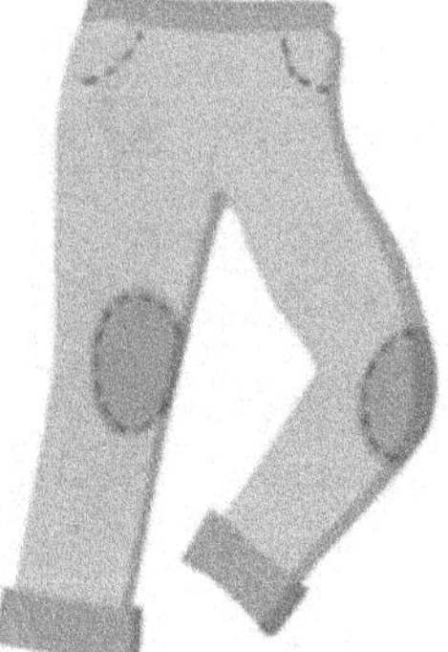

The trousers look like jeans.

slip

زیر شلوار

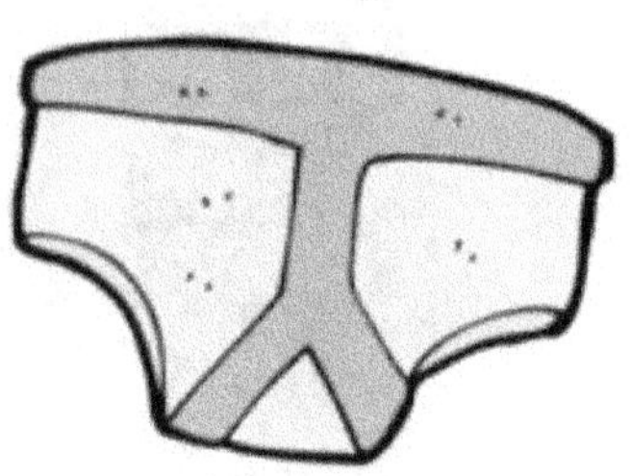

I always wear my underwear.

maillot de corps

زیر لباس

My undershirt has a star.

une

یکی

Number one and the bee are friends.

deux

دو

The cat and the mouse both love two.

trois

سه

The bear gives number three a present.

quatre

چهار

Number four is a home for the cat.

cinq

پنج

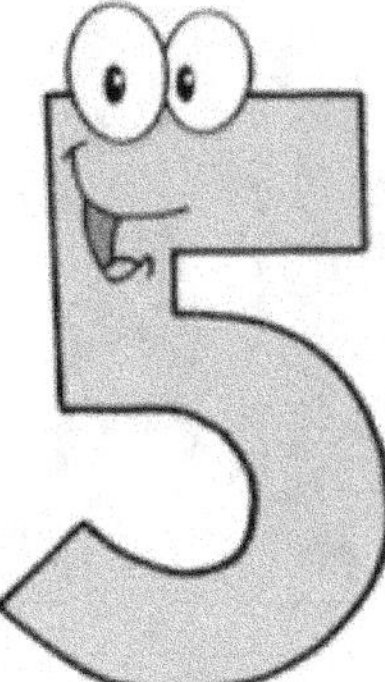

Number five hatches an egg.

six

شش

Number six is going to eat a carrot.

sept

هفت

Number seven is playing with the tiger.

huit

هشت

Number eight is funny.

neuf

نه

Number nine meets the parrot.

dix

ده

Number ten is smiling.

onze

یازده

Number eleven has big eyes.

douze

دوازده

Number twelve is number one and two.

treize

سیزده

Number thirteen is excited.

quatorze

چهارده

The number fourteen is vast.

quinze

پانزده

The number fifteen is green.

seize

شانزده

Sixteen is my lucky number.

dix-sept

هفده

Number seventeen look alike.

dix-huit

هجده

Number eighteen will go to the circus.

dix-neuf

نوزده

I am nineteen now!

vingt

بیست

Number twenty has a zero.

fourmi

مورچه

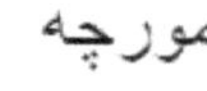

The ant has lots of legs.

cloche

زنگ

The bell will ring.

vache

گاو

The cow has a bow.

poupée

عروسک

She has a cute bear doll.

oeuf

تخم مرغ

The chick has hatched out of the egg.

poisson

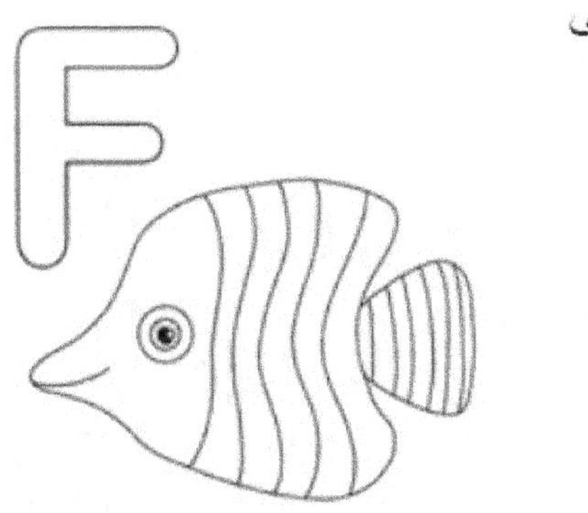

ماهی

The fish is swimming in the water.

chèvre

بز

The goat is sitting on the grass.

chapeau

کلاه

He is wearing a hat.

crème glacée

بستنی

I like to eat ice cream.

confiture

مربا

The kitten is sitting on the jam jar.

chaton

بچه گربه

The cat is sleeping on the floor.

lion

شیر نر

The lion is waiting for the tiger.

rat

موش

The mouse has lots of presents.

nez

بینی

The reindeer has a red nose.

hibou

جغد

The owl is sleeping.

porc

خوک

The pig will eat cupcakes.

reine

ملکه

The queen has a big crown.

lapin

خرگوش

The rabbit is jumping up and down.

mouton

گوسفند

The sheep have fluffy wool.

tortue

لاک پشت

The turtle has a shell.

parapluie

چتر

The mouse is holding an umbrella.

van

ون

The van is driving along the road.

pastèque

هندوانه

The watermelon has lots of seeds.

xylophone

xylophone

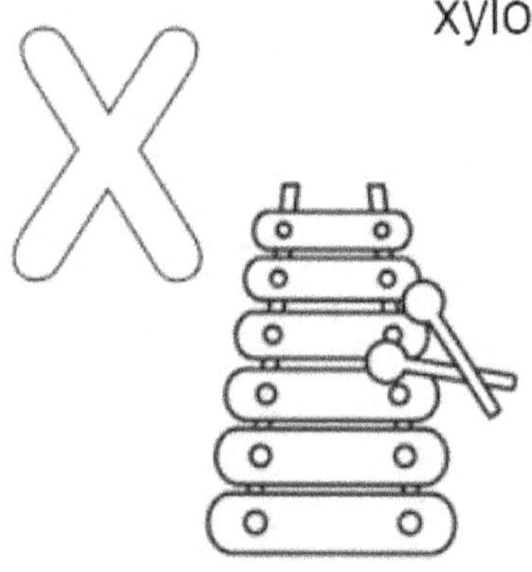

We are going to play the xylophone.

yaourt

ماست

We opened the yogurt can.

zèbre

گورخر

The zebra is surprised.

rose

رنگ صورتی

color the word and
the picture in pink

Most of my clothes are pink.

marron

رنگ قهوه ای

color the word and
the picture in pink

brown

My chocolate is brown.

gris

خاکستری

color the word and
the picture in pink

gray

I don't like the color gray.

vert

سبز

color the word and
the picture in pink

green

The vegetables are green.

jaune

رنگ زرد

color the word and
the picture in pink

yellow

Bananas are yellow.

blanc

سفید

color the word and
the picture in pink

white

The paper that I write on is white.

rouge

قرمز

color the word and
the picture in pink

red

Apples are red.

bleu

آبی

The night sky is blue.

percer

مته

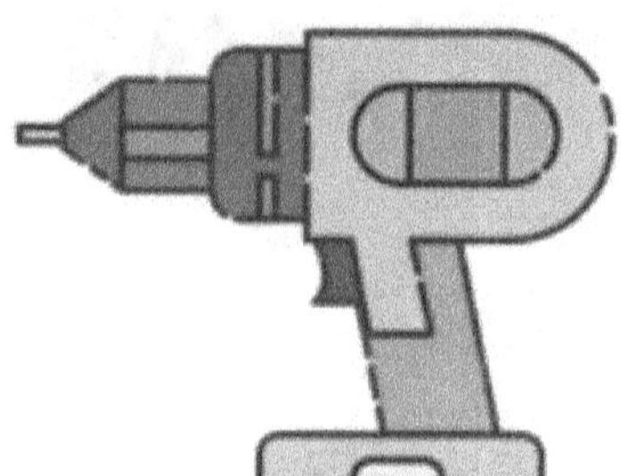

The drill will help us fix this.

marteau

چکش

The hammer is going to nail the picture.

couteau

چاقو

The knife is sharp.

pinces

انبر

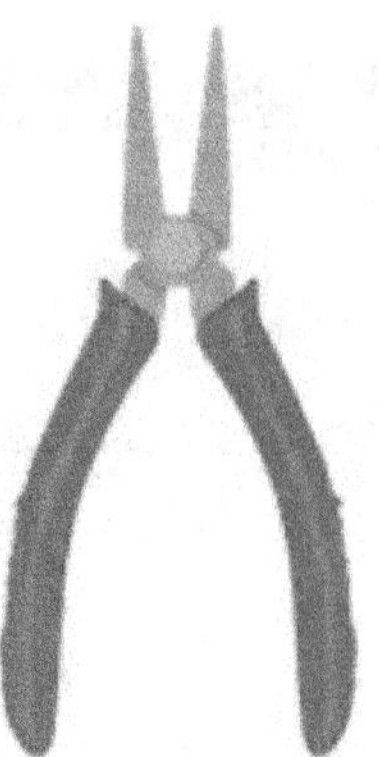

The plier is used for many things.

vu

اره

The saw can chop wood.

les ciseaux

قیچی

I use scissors to cut paper.

tournevis

پیچ گوشتی

The screwdriver can screw in the knots.

clé

آچار

The wrench can help unscrew the knots.

avion

هواپیما

The airplane is going to leave now.

vélo

دوچرخه

The bicycle is beautiful.

bateau

قایق

The boat is floating on the water.

autobus

اتوبوس

The bus is going to school.

voiture

ماشین

The car is green.

hélicoptère

بالگرد

The helicopter is looking for something.

cheval

اسب

You can ride the horse.

jet

جت

The jet is high-speed.

moto

موتورسیکلت

The motorcycle is on the road.

navire

كشتى

The ship is on the water.

métro

مترو

My mom goes on the subway to work.

taxi

تاكسى

The taxi has someone inside.

train

قطار ـ تعليم دادن

The train is going slowly.

un camion

كاميون

The truck has stuff in it.

asperges

مارچوبه

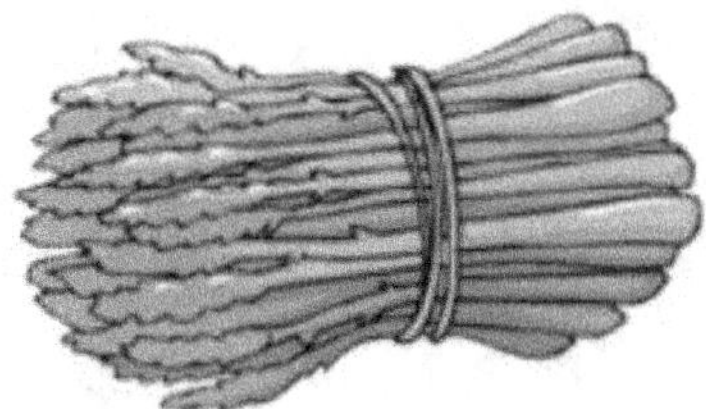

The asparagus is in a bundle.

des haricots

لوبيا

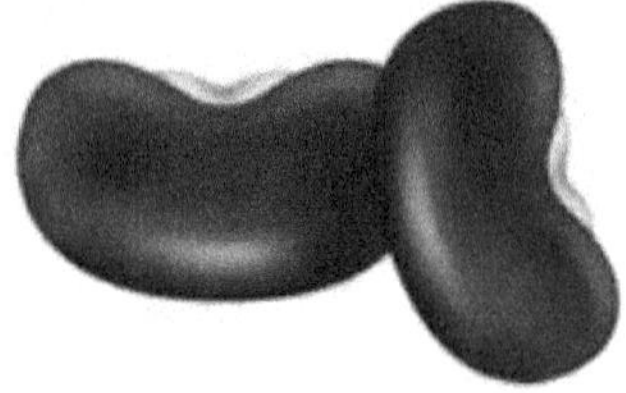

The beans are smooth.

brocoli

كلم بروكلى

The broccoli is dancing.

chou

كلم

Bunnies like to eat cabbage.

carotte

هويج

The carrots are very long.

céleri

كرفس

The celery has lots of leaves.

blé

ذرت

Corn soup is delicious.

concombre

خیار

The cucumbers are cut into pieces.

aubergine

بادمجان

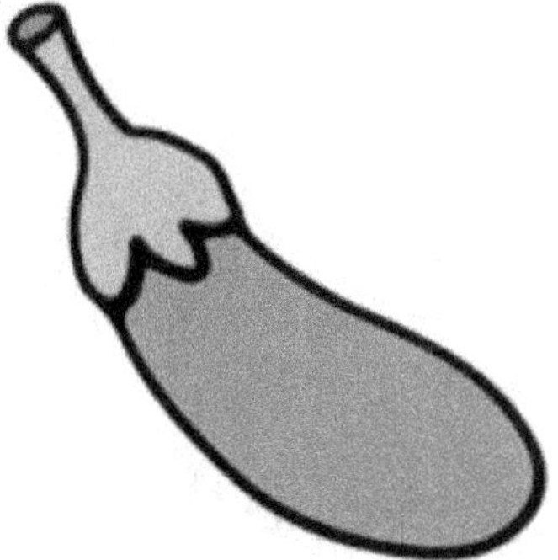

The eggplant is purple.

poivre vert

فلفل سبز

The green pepper is juicy.

salade

كاهو

The lettuce is all green.

oignon

پیاز

The onions make my eyes water.

pois

نخود فرنگی

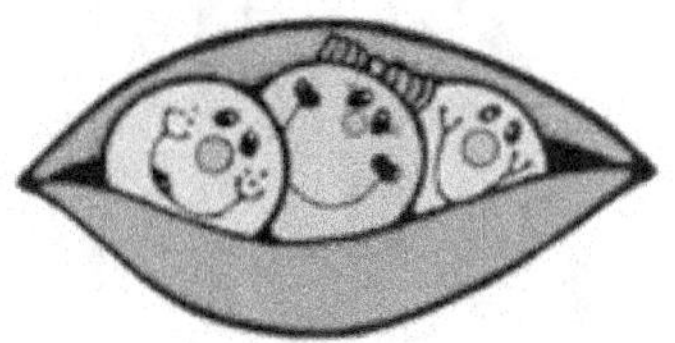

The peas are all in a pod.

patate

سیب زمینی

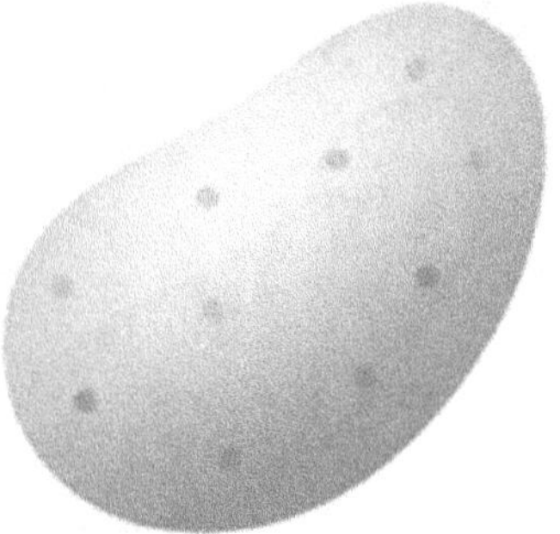

The potato is very shiny.

citrouille

کدو تنبل

The pumpkin is for Halloween.

un radis

تربچه

The radish is a type of vegetable.

épinard

اسفناج

The spinach is good with cheese.

patate douce

سیب زمینی شیرین

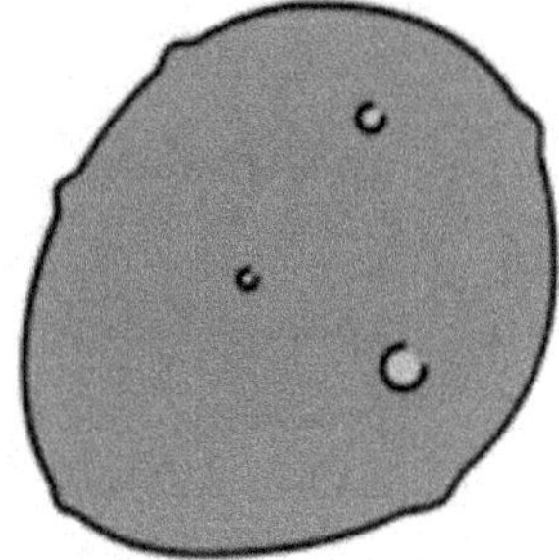

The sweet potato is quite sweet.

tomate

گوجه فرنگی

I don't like to eat tomatoes.

navet

شلغم

My mom bought some turnips.

nuageux

ابری

The weather is cloudy today.

du froid

سرما

I like cold weather.

cool

سرد

The temperature is cold today.

brumeux

مه آلود

The fog is so strong I can't see the city.

chaud

داغ

The fire is burning hot.

humide

مرطوب

It's so humid and wet today.

pluvieux

بارانی

It's raining very hard.

neigeux

برفی

Welcome to snow land!

orageux

طوفانی

I hate the stormy weather.

ensoleillé

آفتابی

The sun is shining!

chaud

گرم

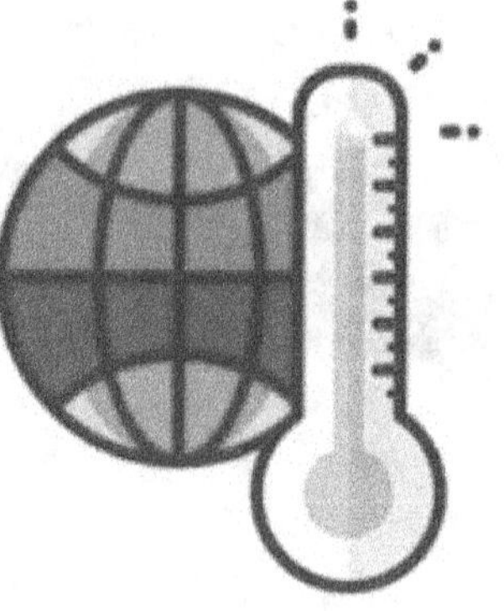

The whole world is warm today!

venteux

بادی

The leaves are blowing away since it's so windy!

tante

عمه

My aunt is very nice to me.

frère

برادر

My brother is very fun to play with.

cousin

عمو زاده

I love going to the playground with my cousin.

fille

فرزند دختر

I like to read books with my daughter.

père

پدر

My father is playing with me.

petite fille

نوه

My granddaughter has blond hair.

grand-mère

مادر بزرگ

My grandmother is very old and has glasses.

petit fils

نوه پسر

My grandson and I are very excited today!

mère

مادر

My mother likes to pick me up.

neveu

پسر خواهر یا برادر

My father's nephew is my cousin.

nièce

دختر برادر یا خواهر و غیره

My niece is very good at playing ball.

sœur

خواهر

My sister is so pretty!

fils

فرزند پسر

My son likes to play with toy cars.

belle fille

ناپدری

My stepdaughter likes the color orange.

belle-mère

مادر خوانده

My stepmother is pretty.

beau-fils

پسر خوانده

This is my stepson, Greg.

oncle

عمو یا دایی

My uncle tells lots of funny jokes.

bol

كاسه

The bowl has nothing inside.

tasse

فنجان

My mom drinks her coffee out of a cup.

plat

ظرف

That dish has a bone inside.

fourchette

چنگال

We have more spoons than forks.

verre

شیشه

I have a glass of water on my desk.

couteau

چاقو

I have a knife in my kitchen.

agresser

لیوان

This mug of coffee is for my dad.

serviette de table

دستمال

You can use the napkins to clean your hands.

poivre

فلفل

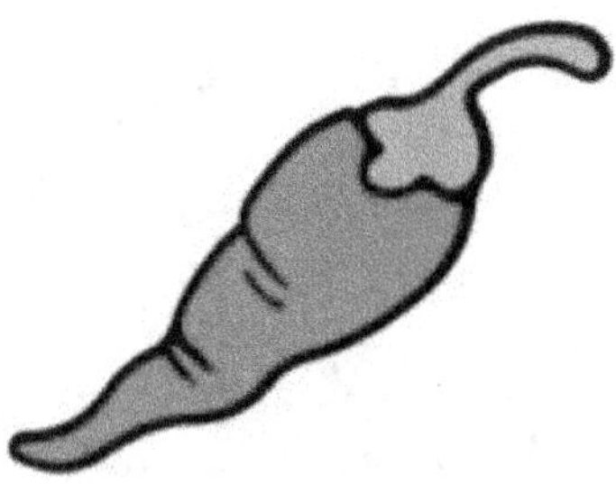

The pepper is very spicy.

lanceur

پارچ

Pour yourself some lemonade from the pitcher.

assiette

بشقاب

Can you help me wash the plates?

salade

سالاد

The salad is very healthy for you.

sel

نمک

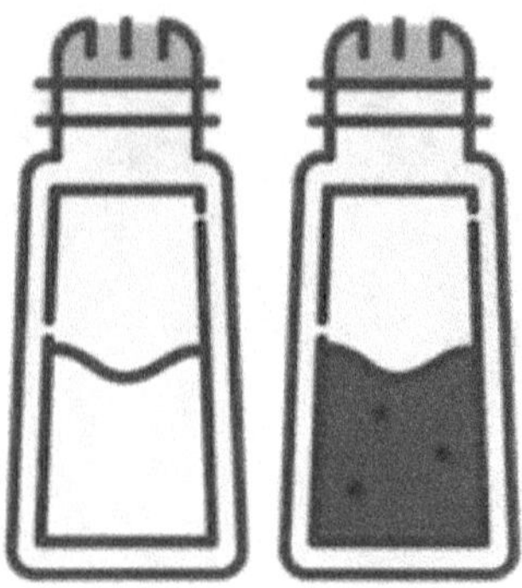

The salt tastes good with a few pinches of pepper.

soucoupe

نعلبکی

The plate is for my cup.

cuillère

قاشق

I use a spoon to eat my rice.

sucre

قند

The pack of sugar is very heavy.

dimanche

یکشنبه

Sunday

Sunday is the day to go to Church!

lundi

دوشنبه

Monday

Monday is the day to start school.

mardi

سه‌شنبه

Tuesday

We will go to the shops on Tuesday.

mercredi

چهار شنبه

Wednesday

Wednesday is hard to spell!

jeudi

پنج شنبه

Thursday

Thursday is the fourth day of the week!

vendredi

جمعه

Friday

My birthday is on Friday!

samedi

شنبه

Saturday

Saturday is the weekend!

cuire

پخت

The chef will bake a cake.

ébullition

جوشیدن

I will boil the eggs.

griller

برنج

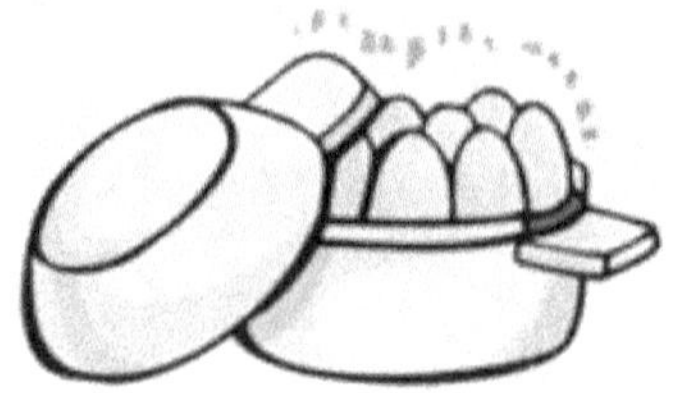

Broil is very yummy.

ouvre-boîte

در بازکن

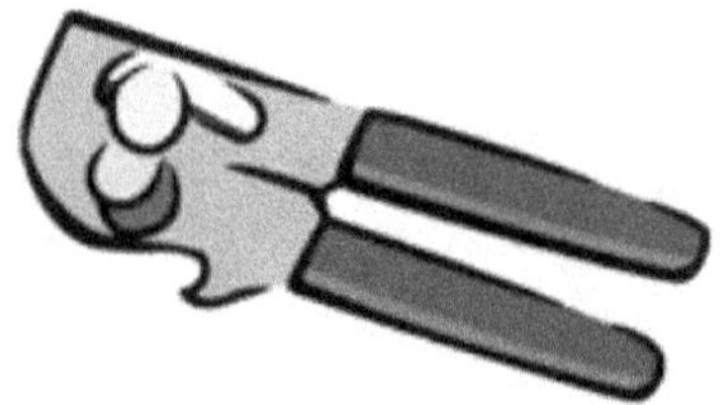

That can opener is used for
opening cans.

frire

سرخ کردن

The pan can fry lots of things.

gril

کوره

We have a grill in our backyard.

tasse à mesurer

جام اندازه گیری

My mom uses the measuring cup
for baking.

cuillère à mesurer

قاشق اندازه گیری

I use a measuring spoon to eat my dessert.

four micro onde

مایکروویو

The microwave is used to heat food.

bol à mélanger

کاسه مخلوط کردن

She is using the mixing bowl to mix things.

serviettes en papier

دستمال توالت

Dry your hands with paper towels.

poché aux œufs

طعم دهنده تخم مرغ

The poach is put on noodles.

porte pot

نگهدارنده گلدان

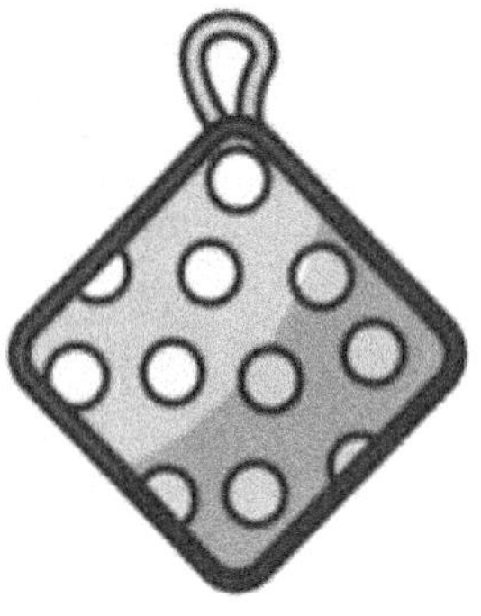

The potholder is soft.

yeux

چشم ها

The eyes are blue.

pieds

پا

I have one pair of feet.

des doigts

انگشتان

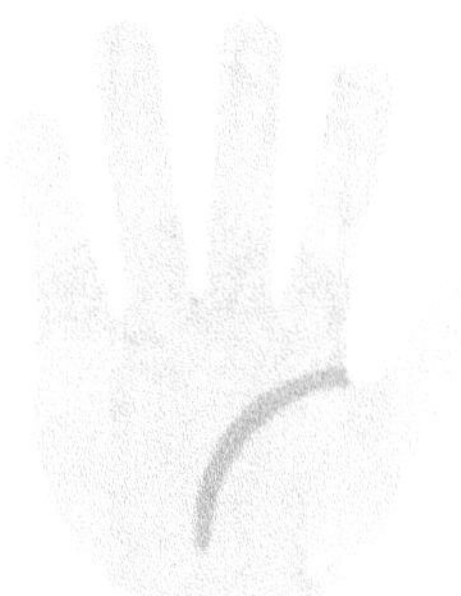

The fingers are waving at us.

pied

پا

My foot has five fingers.

front

پیشانی

My brain is behind my forehead.

cheveux

مو

My hair is long and black.

mains

دست ها

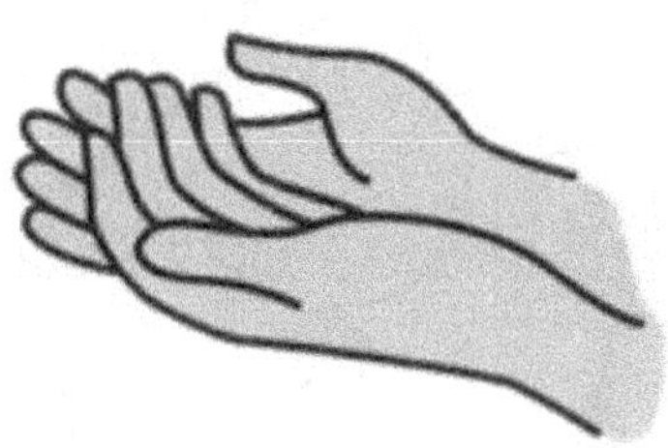

I will wash my hands in the sink.

tête

سر

She has a big head.

les hanches

باسن

The gorilla has his hands on his hips.

les genoux

زانو

She is begging on her knees.

jambes

پاها

The tiger has strong legs.

lèvres

لب

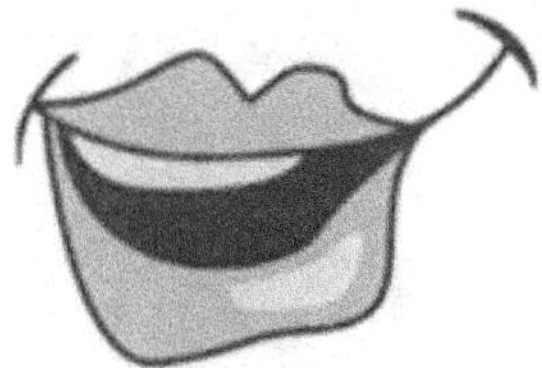

The lips have lipstick on.

bouche

دهان

He is covering his mouth with his hand.

cou

گردن

The necklace is very special to me.

nez

بینی

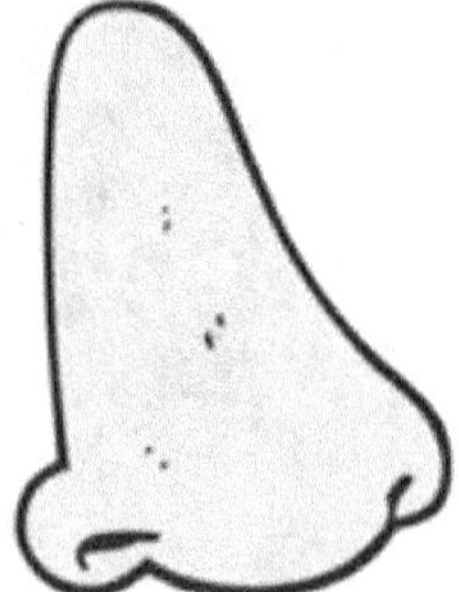

The nose smells something.

épaules

شانه ها

He puts his hands on his shoulders.

estomac

معده

He has a big stomach.

les dents

دندان

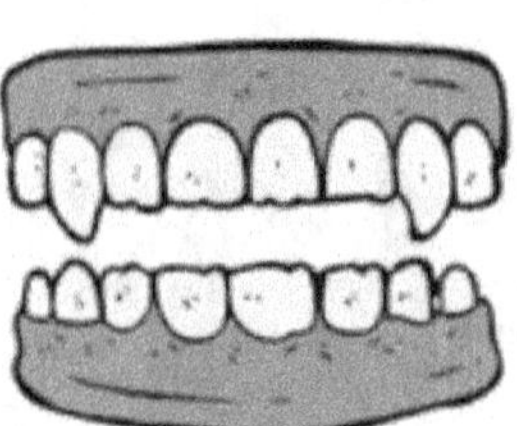

The teeth are clean and white.

gorge

گلو

He has a sore throat today.

les orteils

انگشتان پا

My toes are small.

langue

زبان

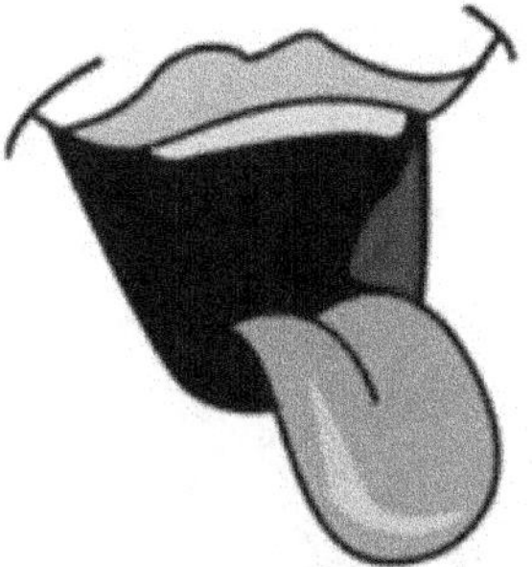

My tongue is licking ice cream.

dent

دندان

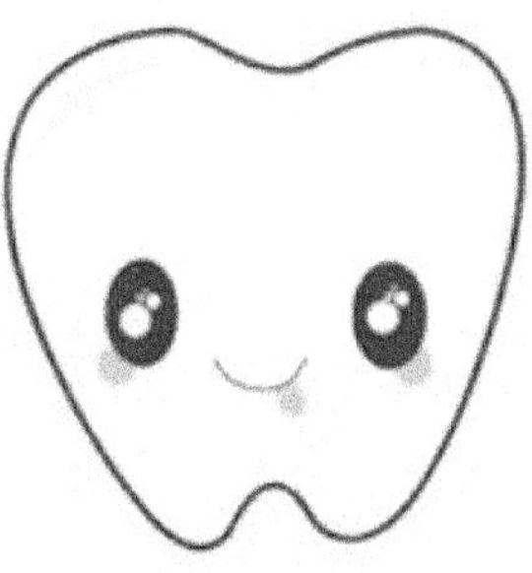

The tooth has big eyes.

taille

کمر

He has his hands on his waist.

salopette

لباس

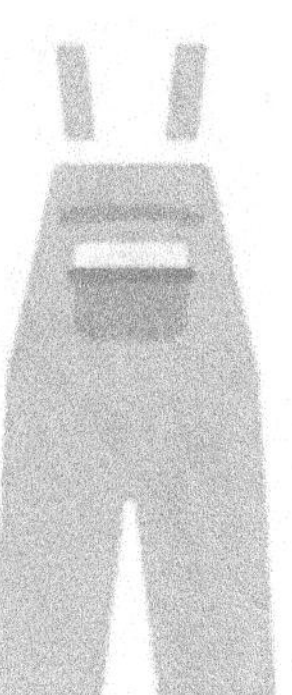

I bought these overalls for you!

mitaines

دستکش

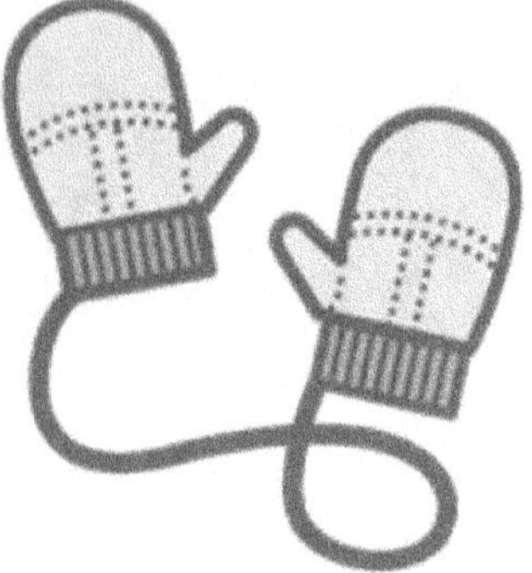

The mittens are very warm.

bonnet

بانی

The beanie is for winter.

tablier

پیشبند

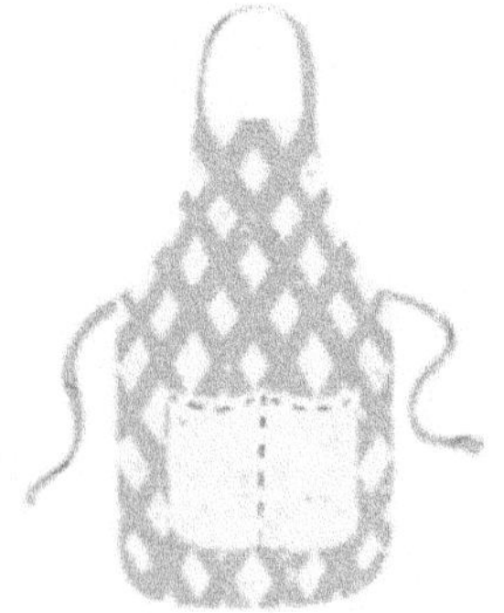

I wear my apron when I bake.

poupée

عروسک

The doll is for my baby sister.

hochets

تکان خوردن

The rattle is for the baby.

jouet

اسباب بازی

The toy is very fun.

couche

پوشک

The baby has to wear a diaper.

berceau

باسینت

She is sleeping in her bassinet.

bavoir

بی بی

My baby brother has to wear his bib when he is eating.

octogone

هشت وجهی

The octagon is saying okay!

triangle

مثلث

The triangle has three corners.

carré

مربع

Square

The square has four sides.

cercle

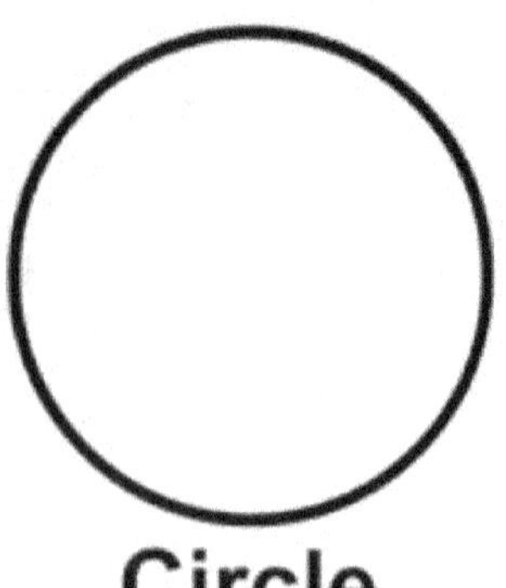

دايره

Circle

The circle is round.

ovale

بيضى

The oval shape looks like a circle.

cœur

قلب

I drew a heart on my paper.

traverser

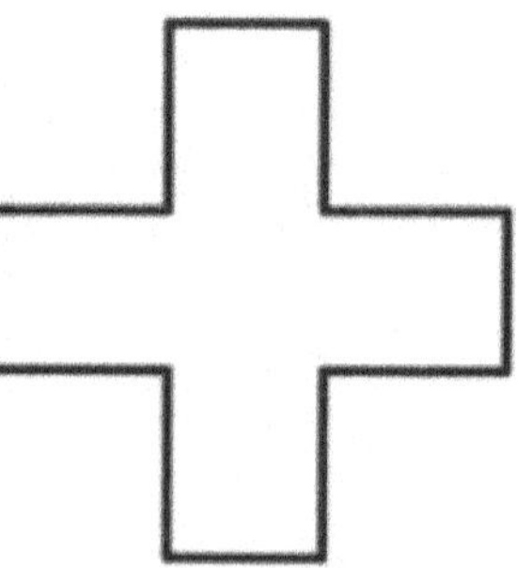

صليب

That sign is a cross.

la flèche

فلش

The arrow is pointing this way.

cube

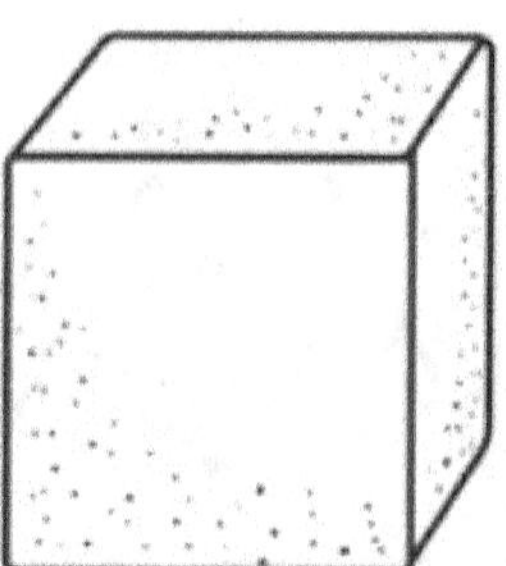

مكعب

The cube is 3D.

étoile

ستاره

The star is yellow and shiny.

tir à l'arc

تیراندازی با کمان

The archery is where you aim.

badminton

بدمینتون

My favorite sport is badminton.

criquet

کریکت

I am very good at cricket.

bowling

بولینگ

I got one pin down at bowling!

boxe

بوکس

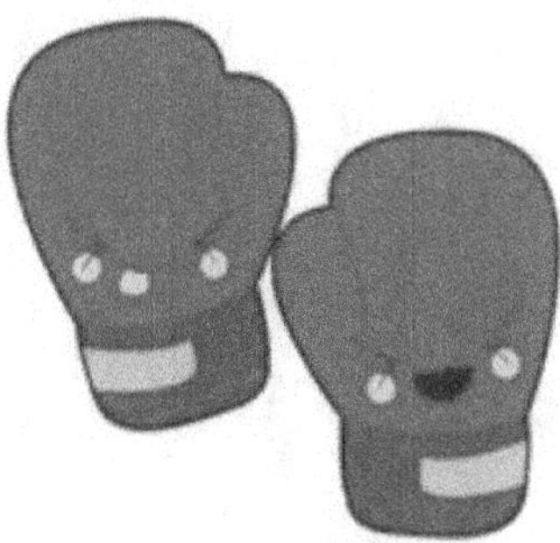

The boxing gloves are hot.

tennis

تنیس

He can hit the ball in tennis.

faire de la planche a roulettes

ورزش اسکیت بورد

He skateboards to school.

planche de surf

تخته موج سواری

The shark loves surfing in the ocean.

le hockey

هاکی

I like to play Ice hockey.

yoga

یوگا

He is closing his eyes and doing yoga.

épée

شمشیر بازی

They are fencing and dueling together.

aptitude

تناسب اندام

She will do some fitness in the pool.

gymnastique

ژیمناستیک

He can do brilliant gymnastics.

karaté

کاراته

She is good at kicking in Karate.

volley-ball

والیبال

She is holding a volleyball.

musculation

وزنه برداری

The girl with brown hair can do weightlifting.

basketball

بسکتبال

He can balance the ball with one finger in basketball.

base-ball

بیسبال

The little chick is in the finales at baseball.

le rugby

راگبی

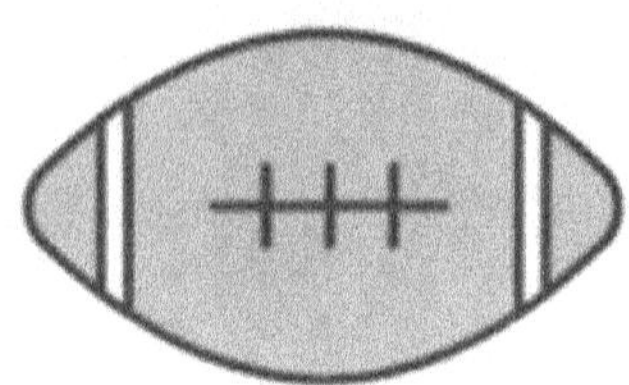

The rugby ball has white stripes.

lutte

کشتی

The sumo will compete in wrestling.

course de voitures

مسابقات اتومبیل رانی

He is number one for car racing.

cyclisme

دوچرخه سواري

He is peacefully cycling on the road.

fonctionnement

در حال دويدن

He is running while listening to his earphones.

tennis de table

تنیس روی میز

My brother and dad will play table tennis.

pêche

صید ماهی

He will go to the river to fish.

judo

جودو

She has a red belt in Judo.

escalade

سنگ نوردی

He will climb the ladder.

tournage

تیراندازی کردن

He is shooting the archery board.

le golf

گلف

She is going to compete in the golf competition.

balade

سوار شوید

He will ride his scooter.

asseyez-vous

بنشین

They are sitting down together.

se lever

بایستید

She likes to stand up.

bats toi

مبارزه کردن

They are fighting over the book.

rire

خنده

He is laughing so hard!

lis

خواندن

She read a picture book.

jouer

بازی

He went to play on the slide.

ecoutez

گوش کنید

He listened for the ice cream cart.

pleurer

گریه کردن

He cried because he got a bad grade.

pense

فکر

He thought that the test would be hard.

chanter

آواز خواندن

He sang for the concert.

regarder la télévision

تلویزیون را تماشا کنید

He watched TV the whole night.

danse

رقص

She was a good dancer.

allumer

روشن کن

The light is turned on.

éteindre

خاموش کنید

The light is turned off.

gagner

پیروزی

He won the contest.

mouche

پرواز

The parrot can fly.

couper

قطع کردن

He was cutting his nails.

désinvolte

دور انداختن

He threw away the garbage.

dormir

خواب

He slept soundly.

fermer

نزدیک

He closed his mouth shut.

ouvert

باز کن

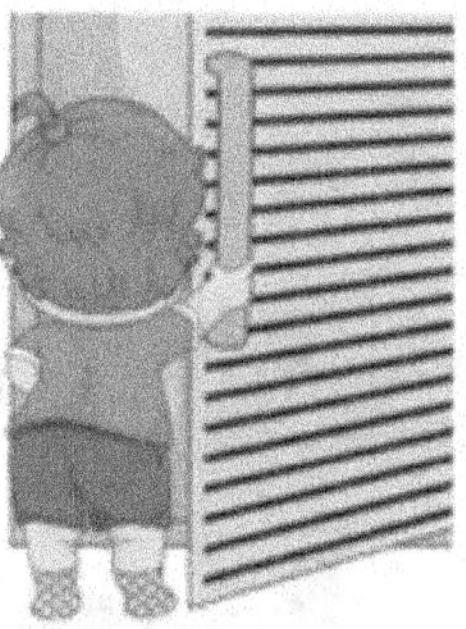

She opened the bathroom door.

écrire

نوشتن

She wrote with a pencil.

donner

دادن

Santa gave her a present.

sauter

پرش

She had fun jumping.

manger

بخور

The shark ate yummy ice cream.

boisson

بنوش

The old British man drank tea.

cuisinier

پختن

The microwave cooked his soup.

lavage

شستشو

You need to remember to wash
your hands.

attendre

صبر کن

He was waiting for the bus.

montée

بالا رفتن

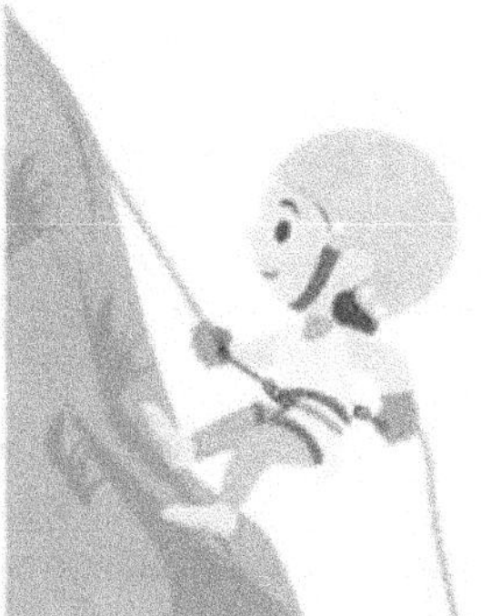

She climbed a lot of mountains.

parler

صحبت

Two best friends were talking together.

crawl

خزیدن

The baby crawled on the floor.

rêver

رویا

The Sloth dreamed about eating leaves.

creuser

حفر کردن

That strong man dug a swimming pool.

taper

کف زدن

The baby clapped her hands.

tricoter

بافتن

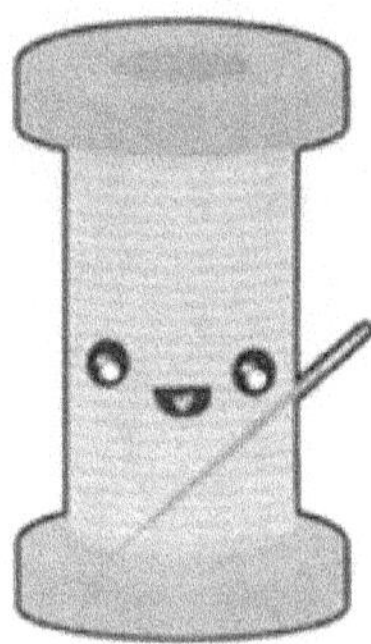

She knits with the purple string.

coudre

دوختن

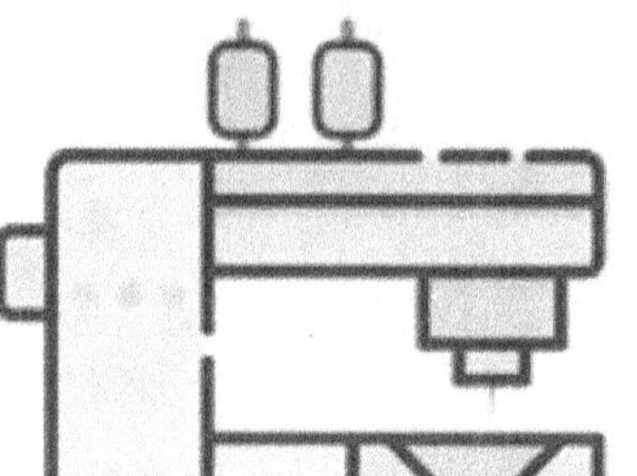

That is a sewing machine.

odeur

بو

The perfume smelled great.

baiser

بوسه

He kissed his mother.

étreinte

در آغوش گرفتن

They hugged each other.

ronfler

خروپف

The tiger snored.

baigner

حمام کردن

He took a bath.

s'incliner

رکوع

He bowed to the judge.

peindre

رنگ

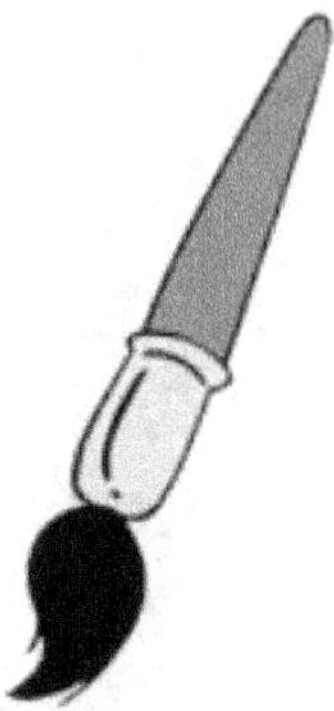

He painted a colorful picture.

se plonger

شیرجه رفتن

He dove to the deepest part of the ocean.

ski

اسکی

The ski was expensive.

empiler

پشته

The books are stacked high.

acheter

خرید

They bought cereal.

secouer

تکان دادن

They shook hands together.

programmeur

برنامه نویس

He was a smart computer programmer.

vétérinaire

دامپزشکی

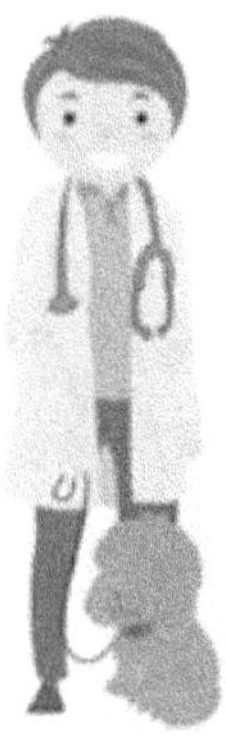

She is a veterinarian.

vendeur de rue

فروشنده خیابانی

That street vendor sells hot dogs.

mineur

معدن کار

That Miner will find gold.

prof

معلم

The owl is the teacher.

groom

باربر، پیشخدمت

That Bellboy is fat.

orateur

بلندگو

The chicken is a great Speaker.

boucher

قصاب

The Butcher sells fish.

pharmacien

داروساز

That Pharmacist saved a person's life.

réceptionniste

مسئول پذیرش

He is a Receptionist.

politicien

سیاستمدار

He wants to be a Politician.

guide touristique

راهنمای تور

That Tour guide led us around Japan.

entrepreneur

کارآفرین

He is an Entrepreneur.

danseuse de ballet

رقصنده باله

She is training to be a Ballet dancer.

astronaute

فضانورد

He is a great astronaut.

juge

قاضی

That Judge is always fair.

avocat

وکیل

The lawyer is serious.

la caissière

صندوقدار

She is a cashier at the market.

conducteur de taxi

راننده تاکسی

He is a fast Taxi driver.

plombier

لوله کش

That Plumber fixes toilets.

musicien

نوازنده

She wants to be a Musician like
her teacher.

chef

سرآشپز

The chef makes fast food.

boulanger

بیکر

That baker is a bread.

artiste

هنرمند

That Artist came from Italy.

acteur

بازیگر

That actor is famous.

barman

پارس

The Bartender works in a bar.

coiffeur

آرایشگاه

That girl is a Hairdresser.

évêques

اسقفها

He is a Bishop.

opticien

عینک فروشی

She went to an Optician.

fleuriste

گلدار

She is a great Florist.

écrivain

نویسنده

He is a famous author.

comptable

حسابدار

My accountant is loyal.

du vin

شراب

That wine tastes good.

café

قهوه

That coffee is bitter.

limonade

لیموناد

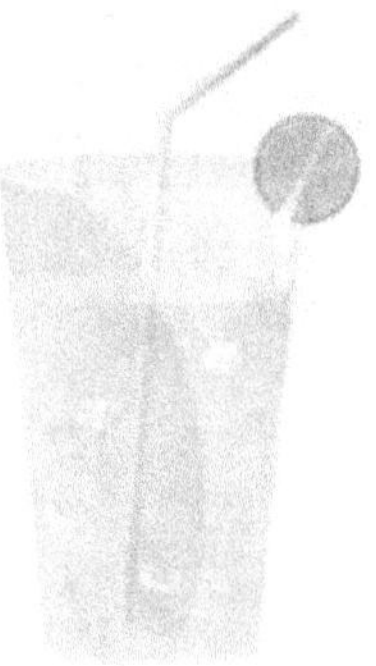

The lemonade is refreshing.

chocolat chaud

شکلات داغ

I drink hot chocolate every day.

milk-shake

میلکشیک

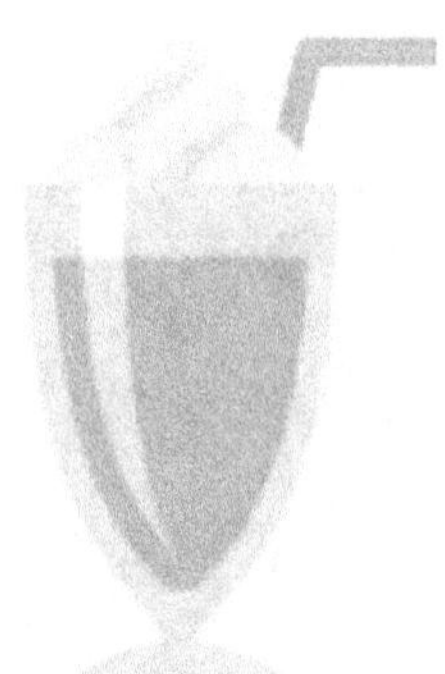

The milkshake has whipped cream.

eau

اب

The water is not cold.

thé

چای

The tea is hot.

lait

شیر

Milk is white.

bière

آبجو

The beer is foamy.

un soda

جوش شیرین

The soda is fizzy.

smoothie

اسموتی

The smoothie is a watermelon flavor.

milk-shake

میلکشیک

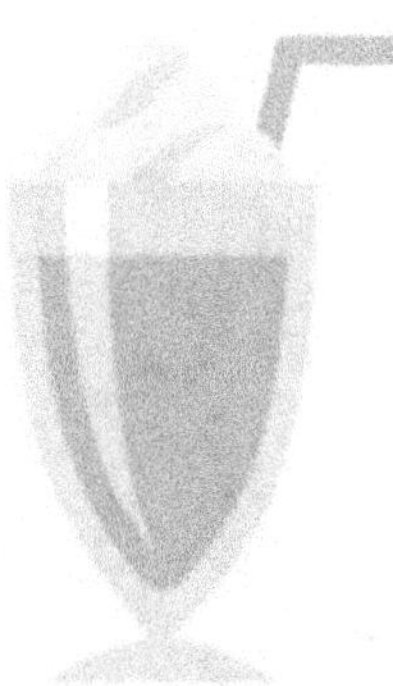

The milkshake has whipped cream.

lait de coco

شیر نارگیل

The coconut milk is yummy.

du jus d'orange

آب پرتقال

The orange juice is made from oranges.

cacao

كاكائو

The cocoa is sweet.

fromage

پنیر

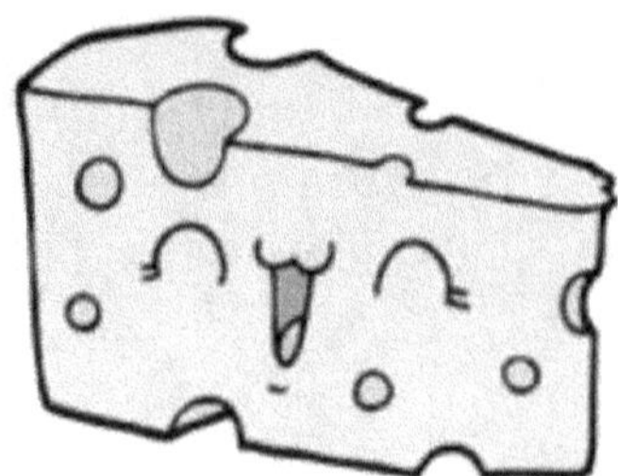

The cheese is creamy.

oeuf

تخم مرغ

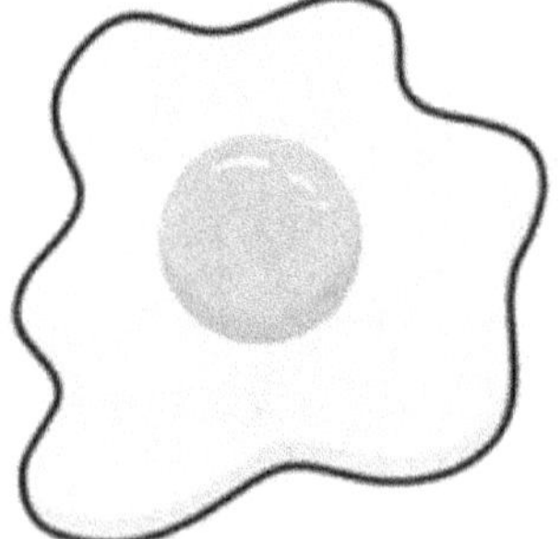

The egg is fried.

beurre

كره

The butter is put on bread.

margarine

مارگارین

Margarine looks like butter.

yaourt

ماست

That yogurt is popular.

cottage cheese

پنیر کلم

The cottage cheese is put on crackers.

crème glacée

بستنی

They have a triple scoop ice cream.

crème

کرم رنگ

That is a lot of creams.

sandwich

ساندویچ

That sandwich is healthy.

saucisse

سوسیس

Americans love sausages.

hamburger

همبرگر

That hamburger looks happy.

hot-dog

هات داگ

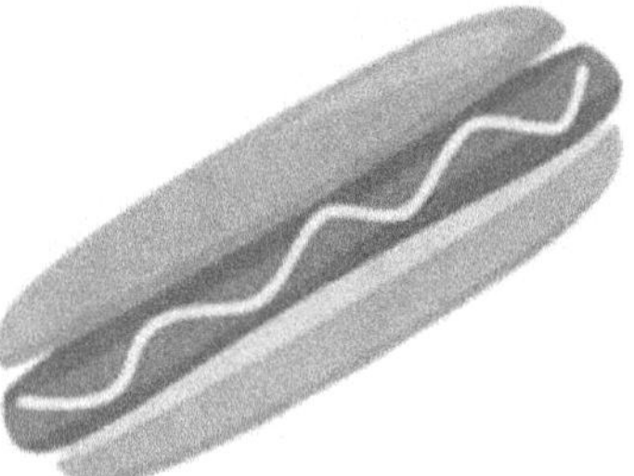

That hot dog has mustard on it.

pain

نان

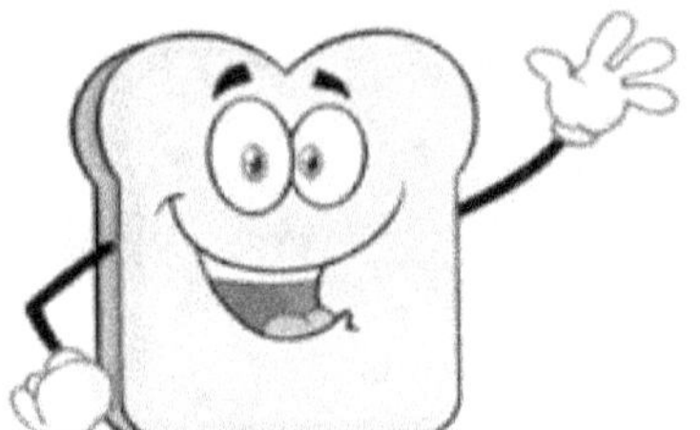

That bread is saying hello.

pizza

پیتزا

That pizza is cheesy.

steak

استیک

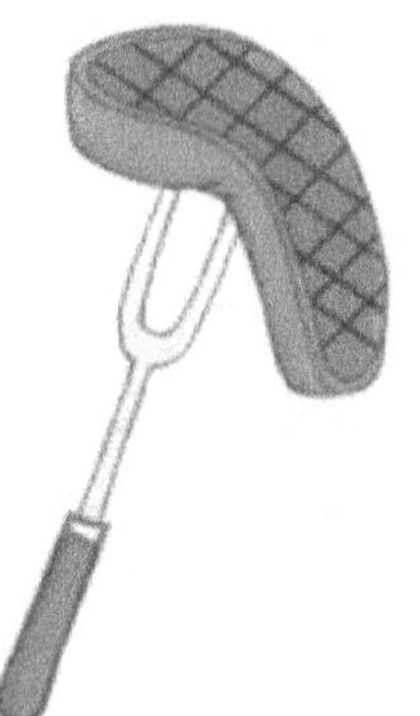

The steak was grilled.

poulet rôti

مرغ سرخ شده

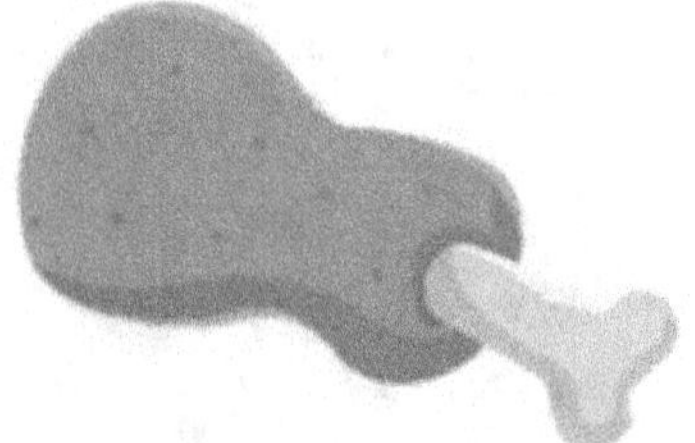

Roast Chicken is delicious.

poisson

ماهی

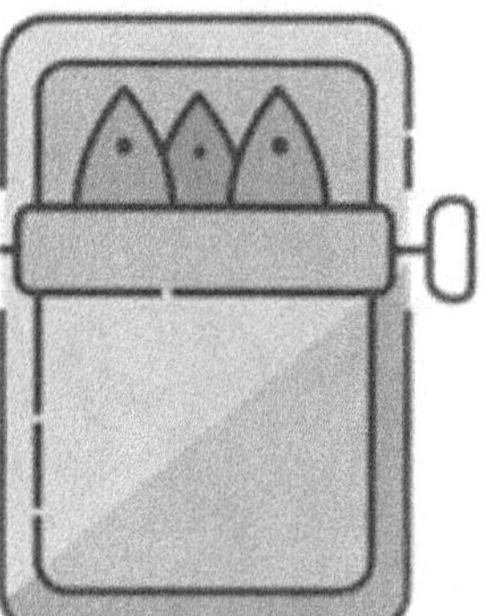

You can buy canned fish in the market.

fruit de mer

غذای دریایی

Lobster is expensive seafood.

jambon

ژامبون

Ham can be put in sandwiches.

kebab

کباب

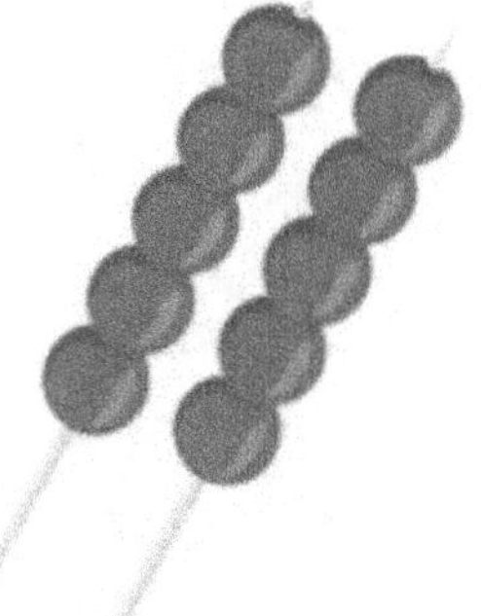

Kebab is a delicacy in America.

bacon

بیکن

That bacon is smiling.

crème fraîche

خامه ترش

You can dip your chips in sour cream.

vache

گاو

Cows are black and white.

lapin

خرگوش

That rabbit is fun to play with.

canard

اردک

That duck is content.

crevette

میگو

The shrimp has six legs.

porc

خوک

That pig is pink and fat.

abeille

زنبور عسل

The bee has a stinger.

chèvre

بز

That goat has a white horn.

crabe

خرچنگ

The crab has two big pincers.

cerf

گوزن

That deer is sleeping.

dinde

بوقلمون

The turkey has a giant tail.

colombe

کبوتر

That dove is carrying a plant.

mouton

گوسفند

That sheep has fluffy wool.

poisson

ماهی

That fish has colorful fins.

poulet

جوجه

That chicken is waking everybody up.

cheval

اسب

The horse has a red mane.

chaise

صندلی

That wing chair is yellow.

meuble tv

میز تلویزیون

The TV stand can hold books.

canapé

کاناپه

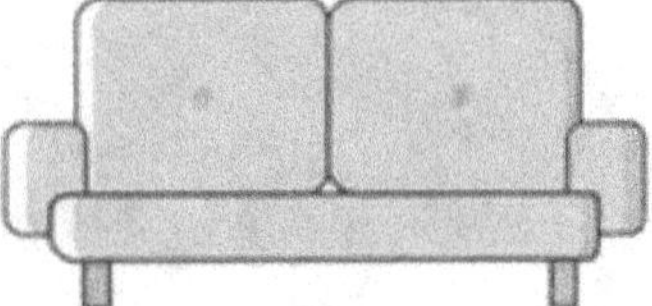

The sofa is comfortable to sit on.

coussins

کوسن ها

The cushion helps soften your seat.

téléphone

تلفن

The telephone is ringing.

télévision

تلویزیون

That television is big.

haut-parleurs

بلندگوها

That speaker is used to increase the volume.

table d'appoint

میز کناری

That end table is sparkling clean.

service à thé

سرویس چای خوری

That tea set is from China.

cheminée

بخاری

The fireplace makes me warm.

télécommandes

از راه دور

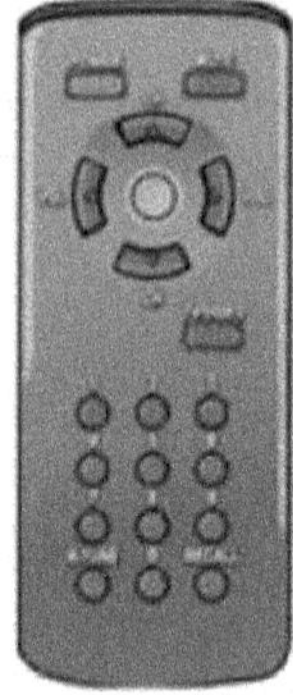

The remote has lots of buttons.

ventilateur électrique

پنکه برقی

The fan is blowing wind.

lampadaire

چراغ پایهدار

The floor lamp is very tall.

tapis

فرش

The carpet is soft and silky.

bureaux

میز

The table is made of wood.

stores

پرده

I will pull the blinds down.

rideaux

پرده ها

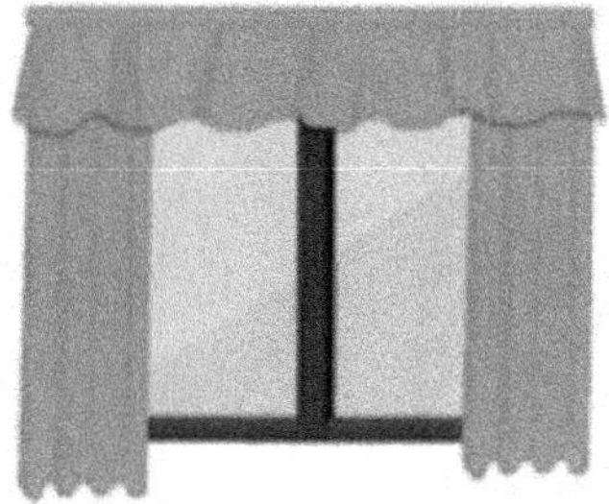

She opened the curtains.

image

تصویر

The picture is about the mountains and the sky.

vase

گلدان

The roses are all in a vase.

l'horloge

ساعت

The alarm clock is beeping.

oreiller

بالش

The pillow is pink and yellow.

cintre

چوب لباسی

The hat stand has only one hat on it.

mettre la table

میز رختکن

I have made up on my dressing table.

lampe de table

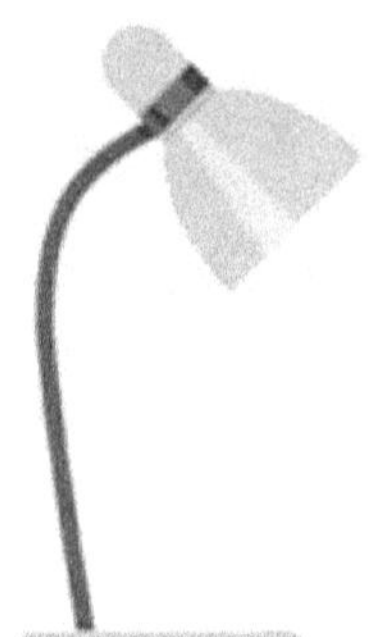

لامپ میز

The table lamp will help me see in the dark.

miroir

آینه

The mirror is very tall.

planche a repasser

تخته اتو

Don't touch the ironing board, it's hot!

boîte avec tiroir

جعبه با کشو

You can keep your clothes in the hope chest.

table de chevet

میز کنار تخت

The nightstand has my lamp on it.

lit

بستر

The bed is charming.

climatisation

تهويه كننده هوا

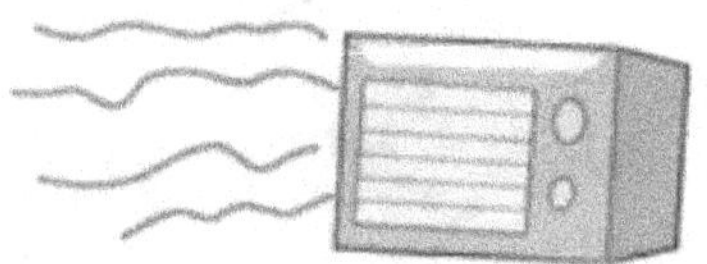

The air conditioner is cold.

cruche

كوزه

The measuring jug has nothing inside.

dentifrice

خمير دندان

The toothpaste is mint flavored.

brosse à dents

مسواک

The toothbrush has toothpaste on it.

savon

صابون

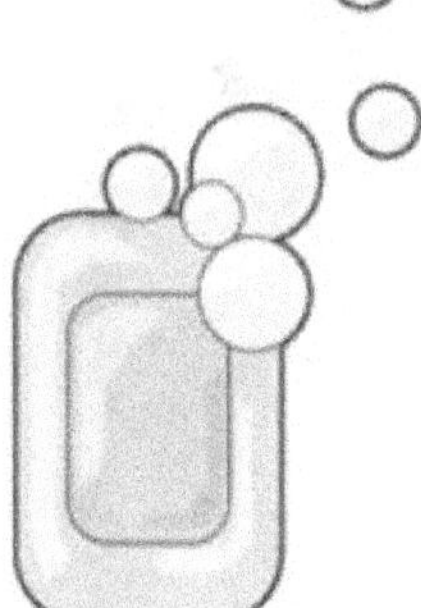

The soap is very bubbly.

pince à linge

لباس

The clothespin will clip my clothes.

cintre

جا رختى

The hanger is hanging my boots.

sèche-cheveux

سشوار

The hairdryer will blow my hair.

shampooing

شامپو

The shampoo is used to clean your hair.

bulle

حباب

The bubbles are very fun to play in.

brosse

قلم مو

She is brushing her hair with the brush.

papier toilette

دستمال توالت

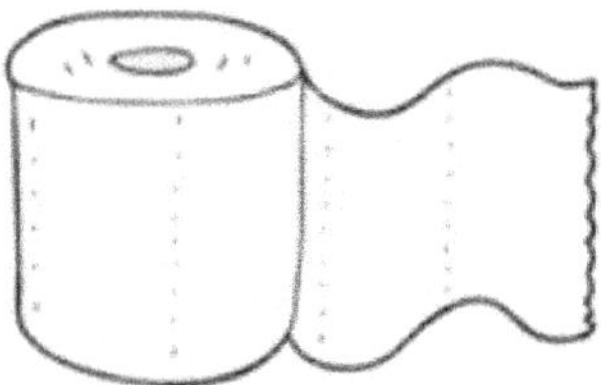

The toilet paper is used to dry your hands.

serviette

حوله

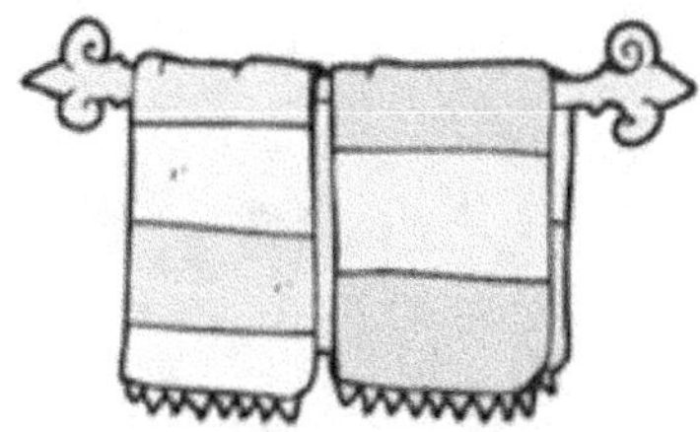

We have two towels on the rack.

corde à linge

خط لباس

My shirt is hanging on the clothesline.

douche

دوش

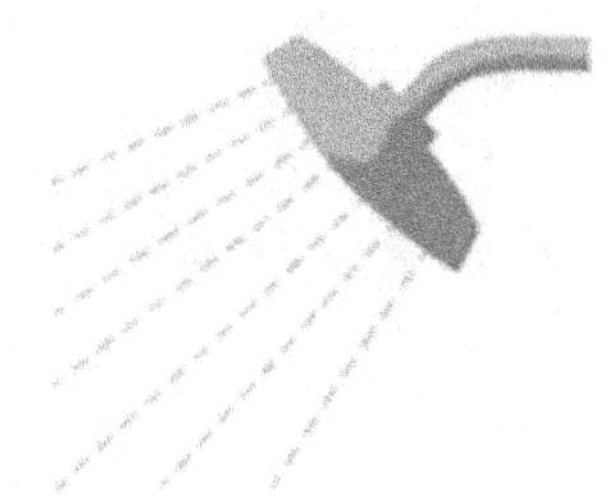

The shower is spraying water.

baignoire

وان

The bathtub is comfortable.

lessive

پودر لباس شویی

The laundry detergent is used with the washing machine.

seau

سطل

Can you help me fill up the bucket?

vadrouilles

مپس

The mop is used for mopping the floor.

savon liquide

صابون مايع

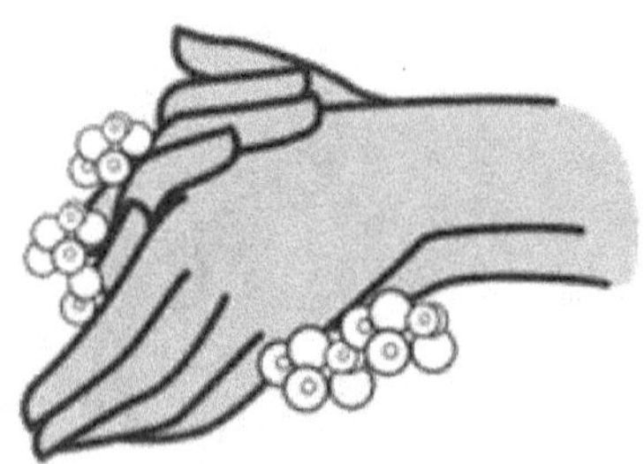

I use soapy water to wash my hands.

lessive en poudre

پودر شستنشو

I will scoop up the washing powder.

sac poubelle

کیسه زباله

The trash bag is full of trash.

poubelle

سطل آشغال

You have only to put recylcle trash in the trash can.

les puits

غرق می شود

You should wash your hands in the sink.

cuvette des toilettes

كاسه توالت

She let her bunny use the toilet.

machine à laver

ماشین لباسشویی

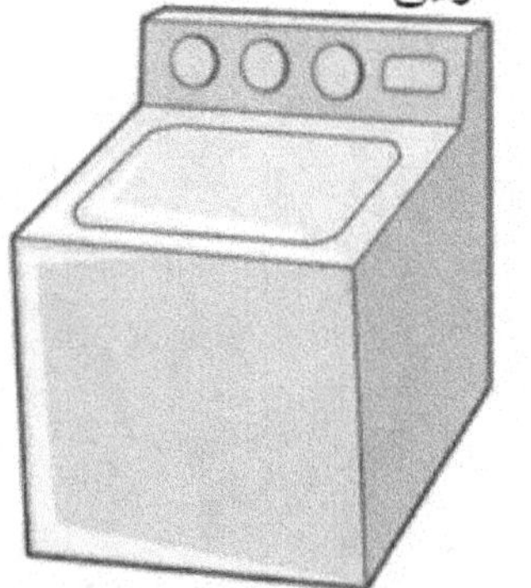

The washing machine wash your clothes.

panier à linge

سبد لباسشویی

She is putting all the clothes into the laundry basket.

le rasoir

تیغ

He uses the razor to shave his beard.

rasoir électrique

تیغ برقی

The electric razor works faster than the normal one.

crème à raser

كرم اصلاح

The shaving cream is fluffy.

bain de bouche

دهانشویه

The mouthwash smells very lovely.

coton-tige

جوانه پنبه

Q-tip can be used for many things.

brosse à cheveux

برس مو

She brushes her hair with her hairbrush.

peigne

شانه

Her dad will comb her hair for her.

nettoyant

پاک کننده

Put the cap back on the cleanser bottle.

échelle

مقیاس

You can measure things on the scale.

papier de soie

دستمال کاغذی

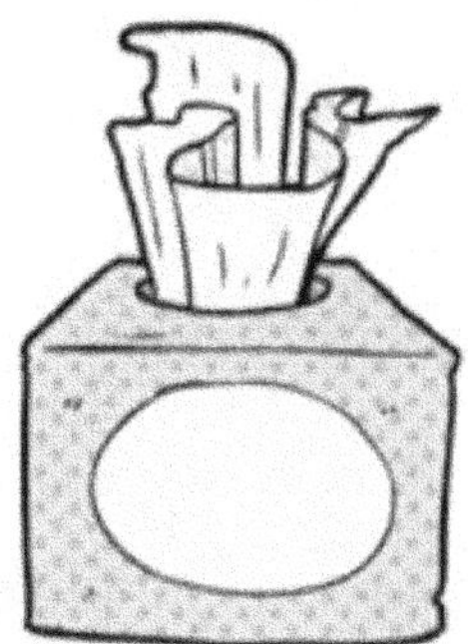

The tissue is on the counter.

jouets de bain

اسباب بازیهای حمام

The little duck is a bath toy.

robinet

شیر آب

The faucet is broken.

miroir

آینه

He is looking in the mirror.

tapis de bain

فرش دستشویی

The bath mat is purple and yellow.